Yellowstone National Park

by Grace Hansen

Abdo
NATIONAL PARKS
Kids

abdopublishing.com

Published by Abdo Kids, a division of ABDO, P.O. Box 398166, Minneapolis, Minnesota 55439.

Printed in China

102017

012018

THIS BOOK CONTAINS RECYCLED MATERIALS

Photo Credits: Alamy, iStock, Library of Congress, Shutterstock, ©User:Partytimeusa p.19/CC-BY-3.0

Production Contributors: Teddy Borth, Jennie Forsberg, Grace Hansen

Design Contributors: Dorothy Toth, Laura Mitchell

Publisher's Cataloging in Publication Data

Names: Hansen, Grace, author.

Title: Yellowstone National Park / by Grace Hansen.

Description: Minneapolis, Minnesota : Abdo Kids, 2018. | Series: National Parks | Includes glossary, index and online resource (page 24).

Identifiers: LCCN 2017943173 | ISBN 9781532104367 (lib.bdg.) | ISBN 9781532105487 (ebook) | ISBN 9781532106040 (Read-to-me ebook)

Subjects: LCSH: United States--Yellowstone National Park--Juvenile literature. | National parks and reserves--Juvenile literature. |Natural history--Juvenile literature.

Classification: DDC 917.87--dc23

LC record available at https://lccn.loc.gov/2017943173

Table of Contents

Yellowstone National Park

Yellowstone National Park is in three states. They are Wyoming, Montana, and Idaho.

It officially became a park on March 1, 1872. President Ulysses S. Grant signed it into law. It was the nation's first national park!

Climate

The park is more than 3,400 square miles (8,806 km^2). It can snow in fall, winter, and spring. Thunderstorms are common in summer months.

Habitats

The park is very beautiful. It is filled with lakes, rivers, mountains, and canyons. It is known for its **geysers** and **hot springs**. Very hot **magma** creates them.

There are many types of trees in the park. Lodgepole pines are the most common. Snowshoe hares rely on this tree for food in winter.

Meadows are filled with wildflowers. Shooting star grows from May to June. Elk are often in the park's meadows.

The Grand Canyon of Yellowstone is the largest canyon in the park. The Yellowstone River flows through it. Yellowstone cutthroat trout are **native** to the river.

Mount Washburn is a good area to see wildlife. Bighorn sheep are often on its slopes. Bison live in its valleys. **Aster** and many other plants grow on it.

Only six kinds of **reptiles** live in the park. The most common is the terrestrial garter snake. It lives near water in all areas of the park.

Fun Activities

Boat or fish in Yellowstone Lake

Cross-country ski or snowshoe in the winter months

Gaze at stunning views in Canyon Village

Visit famous geyser Old Faithful, which erupts every 92 minutes

Glossary

aster – a plant with white, pink, blue, or purple flowers. The flowers are made up of many narrow petals around a yellow center.

geyser – a spring that shoots a stream of hot water, steam, or mud into the air from time to time.

hot spring – a spring of naturally hot water, typically heated by underground volcanic activity.

magma – hot, liquid matter beneath the earth's surface.

native – original to.

reptile – a cold-blooded animal with a skeleton inside its body and dry scales or hard plates on its skin.

Index

Abdo Kids ONLINE

FREE! ONLINE MULTIMEDIA RESOURCES

Visit **abdokids.com** and use this code to access crafts, games, videos, and more!

Abdo Kids Code:
NYK4367